INST

5-STRING

BANJO

by Fred Sokolow.

Oak Publications
New York/London/Sydney

A cassette tape is available that contains all the
tunes and exercises in this book. To order,
send $7.95 to:

Sokolow Music
P.O. Box 491264
Los Angeles, CA 90049

California residents please add applicable sales tax.

Edited by Ronnie Ball
Photography, design and layout by Leonard Vogler
Modelled by Frank Ryan
Instruments kindly loaned by:
Al Sheniger, Guitar & Banjo Workshop, Montrose, PA.
Serge, Sugarman's Musical Instruments, Eynon, PA.
Cover design by Pearce Marchbank

Order No. OK 64741
US ISBN 0.8256.0305.6
UK ISBN 0.7119.0657.2

Exclusive Distributors:
Music Sales Corporation
257 Park Avenue South, New York, NY 10010 USA
Music Sales Limited
8/9 Frith Street, London W1V 5TZ England
Music Sales Pty. Limited
120 Rothschild Street, Rosebery, Sydney NSW 2018 Australia

Printed in the United States of America by
Vicks Lithograph and Printing Corporation

Contents

The Songs

Introduction

Many people have said that the 5-string banjo is the only native American instrument. Actually, the banjo was brought to America by African slaves. But the 5-string was "there" when a lot of music history was made in this country.

- The first blues was strummed on an early, primitive 5-string banjo by plantation slaves.

- The first vaudeville - minstrel music - was inspired by plantation bands playing banjos.

- Ragtime, often called the first jazz, grew out of the rhythms and tonalities of minstrel/banjo music.

- Around the turn of the century, 5-string banjo was as popular a "parlor instrument" as guitar is today. Classical banjoists played first violin parts on the banjo with orchestral backing.

- Southern mountain musicians adopted the banjo and fiddle in the 1800's to play reels, jigs, and ballads.

- In the 1940's, banjo played a key part in the birth of bluegrass music, a synthesis of mountain string band and popular country music.

- Around 1960, banjo was an essential ingredient of the "folk revival." The Weavers, The Kingston Trio, The Limeliters and other folk groups featured the 5-string.

This book surveys the 5-string banjo styles heard today: clawhammer "mountain styles," "folk style" banjo, two- and three-finger picking, and bluegrass. You can use these techniques to play any kind of music you like. Enjoy yourself!

Parts of the Banjo

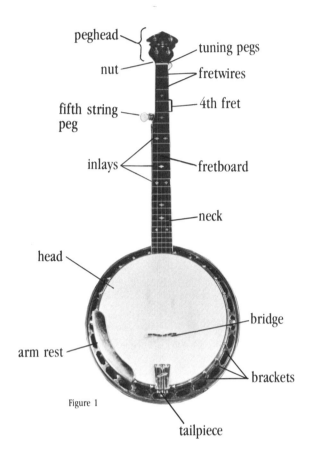

peghead
tuning pegs
nut
fretwires
fifth string peg
4th fret
inlays
fretboard
neck
head
bridge
arm rest
brackets
Figure 1
tailpiece

The strap makes the banjo easier to support. It hooks onto two banjo brackets. Wear it over your right shoulder.

strap
resonator (optional)

Making Some Sound

Strum down on all five strings at once with your thumb, as shown in this picture:

Figure 3

Now, pick just the third string with your thumb.

Fretting a string means pressing it against the fretboard to raise its pitch. Fret the third string/2nd fret, as shown in figure #4 and pick the fretted string with your thumb. A clear note should ring out. If the note is muted or deadened, here are some tips.

- Push the string down harder.

- Use the tip of your finger.

- Press the string down near the fretwire, but not touching it.

Figure 4

Tuning Up

Here's a step-by-step method for getting into G tuning, the tuning most banjo players use:

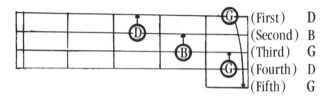

(First)	D
(Second)	B
(Third)	G
(Fourth)	D
(Fifth)	G

- Get a D note from a piano, pitch pipe, guitar (fourth string) or electronic tuner. Tune the fourth string to this note.

- Fret the fourth string at the 5th fret. Pick this note. It's a G.

Figure 5

- Tune the third string to match this G.

- Fret the third string/4th fret and tune the open second string to match it. This is a B.

- Fret the second string/3rd fret and tune the open first string to match it. This is a D.

- Fret the first string/5th fret and tune the open fifth string to match it. This is a G.

Once you're tuned, strum all five strings at once with your thumb; you should hear a G chord.

A Few Easy Chords

When you strum the open (unfretted) banjo strings, you're playing a G chord. Try it. Brush down on all five strings with your thumb in a rapid downward motion.

Now try playing the three chords pictured below. Arch your fingers over the fretboard; each finger should touch only the intended string. Once you've positioned your left hand, strum the chord a few times and make sure each string rings out clearly.

The **grid** beside each picture is a simplified chord diagram — a schematic view of the chord with vertical lines representing the strings and horizontal lines representing the frets.

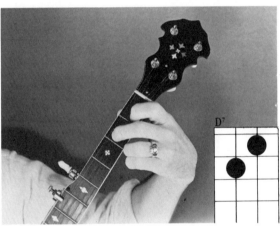

Figure 6

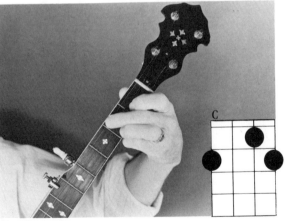

Figure 7

Figure 8

Notice that in all three chords the index finger is fretting the second string/1st fret. When you switch from one chord to another, keep the index finger in place and form the rest of the chord around it.

Try strumming these chord sequences over and over. Strum with your thumb in a slow, steady rhythm. Each slash represents one strum:

G   D⁷   G   D⁷
/ / / / / / / / / / / / / / / /

G   C   G   C
/ / / / / / / / / / / / / / / /

C   F   G   C
/ / / / / / / / / / / / / / / /

G   C   D⁷   G
/ / / / / / / / / / / / / / / /

Strumming A Few Songs

Sing these familiar songs and strum along on the banjo. Keep a steady rhythm and strum once for each slash. The key to success: don't break your right hand rhythm while waiting for your left hand to form a chord; keep strumming in time and make your left hand catch up! Play the rhythm as slowly as you like, but keep it rolling. It's no disaster if you strum a few "klunkers" (chords that didn't quite make it in time for the strum).

WHEN THE SAINTS GO MARCHING IN

```
        G
Oh, when the saints      go marching in,
    /         /   / /    /      /  / /
                                D⁷
Oh, when the saints go marching in,
    /         /      / /    / /  / /
        G                C
Oh Lord, I want   to be in that number,
    /      / /   / /    /         / /
        G         D⁷     G
When the saints go marching in.
    /      /    / /   / /  / /
```

RED RIVER VALLEY

```
            C       G        C
Come and sit by my side if you love me.
  /       / /    / /     /      / /
                        G
Do not hasten to bid me adieu,
  /     / /   /  /   / / /
        C                 F
But remember the Red River Valley
  /      / /     /   /   /    / /
        G                 C
And the cowboy who loves you so true.
  /      / /      /   /    / / /
```

WABASH CANNONBALL

C
Listen to the jingle,
/   /   /   /

             F
the rumble and the roar,
  /   /   /

     G
As she glides along the woodlands,
/   /   /   /   /

                C
through hills and by the shore.
  /   /   /   /

Hear the mighty rush of engines,
    /   /   /

              F
hear the lonesome hoboes call,
/   /   /   /   /

G
Travelin' through the jungles
/   /   /

           C
on the Wabash Cannonball.
/   /   /   /   /

WILL THE CIRCLE BE UNBROKEN

      G
Will the circle   be unbroken
/   / / / / / / /

   C   G
By and By, Lord, by and by.
/   / / / / / /

There's a better   home a-waiting
/   / / / / / / /

         D⁷ G
In the sky, Lord, in the sky.
/ / / / / / / /

SKIP TO MY LOU

C
Lou, Lou, skip to my Lou,
/ / /   /

G
Lou, Lou, skip to my Lou,
/ / /   /

C
Lou, Lou, skip to my Lou,
/ / /   /

G   C
Skip to my Lou, my darling.
/   /   / /

OH, SUSANNA

G   D^7
Oh, I come from Alabama with a banjo on my knee,
/ /   / /   /   /   /   /   /

   G   D^7 G
I'm going to California, my true love for to see.
/   / /   / /   /   /   /

C   G   D^7
Oh, Susanna,   don't you cry for me,
/ / /   / /   /   / /

   G   D^7 G
I'm going to California with my banjo on my knee.
/   / /   /   /   /   /   /

The Basic Strum

Pete Seeger popularized this rhythmic strumming/picking style. You can use it to pick melodies and to accompany singing. It has a **"boom-chick-a"** rhythm:

boom - Pick up on the first string with your index finger. Use the fleshy part of your finger, not the nail.

Figure 9

chick - Brush down on all the strings (especially the first, second and third) with the back (nail) of your middle finger. Keep your middle finger, ring finger and pinkie curled up together before you do this, and brush down by quickly uncurling them.

Figure 10

- **a** -   Pick down on the fifth string with your thumb.

Figure 11

Aim for a galloping, "bumb-ditty" rhythm. Play the three step strum over and over. There should be a pause after "boom," but not after the other two steps. Immediately after your thumb picks the fifth string, your index finger starts the strum over again on the first string.

After you can keep a steady rhythm with the basic strum, add this variation: for step one, pick up on the second string instead of the first . . . still using your index finger. You can also substitute the third or fourth strings. Try them all.

Practice changing chords while doing the basic strum. Try this chord sequence; play it over and over:

strum strum strum strum strum strum strum strum
/   /   /   /   /   /   /   /
G   C   G   D⁷

How to Read Tablature

Next you'll be learning some note-for-note arrangements, so you'll need to know how to read some form of music notation. Instead of standard music notation, you'll be using **tablature**, or tab, because it tells you exactly which strings and frets to play and which right-hand fingers to use. Tab predates regular music notation, and it's the traditional way of writing banjo music.

The five lines of the tablature represent the five banjo strings:

one measure

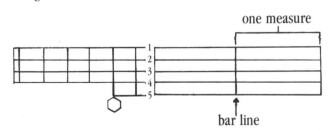

bar line

16

An o on a line tells you to pick the corresponding open (unfretted) string:

A number on a line tells you where to fret a string when you pick it.

Letters under the tab tell you which right-hand finger picks the string:

I = index finger
M = middle finger
T = thumb
B = brush down (with the middle finger or the back of your hand)

Timing: As shown above, tab is divided into **measures** by vertical **bar lines.** Each measure has eight beats. A note whose stem has a flag or is connected to other notes ($\flat$ or $\stackrel{3}{4}$) gets one beat. A note with no flag on its stem ($?$) gets two beats.

Here's how the basic strum looks in tab. Note how the chord letter/names are written above the staff.

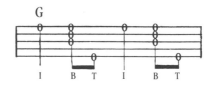

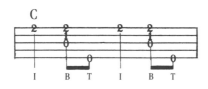

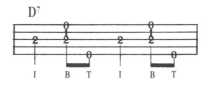

Backing Up Songs with the Basic Strum

The basic strum (Page 14) has a bouncy, rhythmic feel. It makes a perfect accompaniment for songs like the ones on Pages 11, 12, and 13. Try it: play those songs and do one **"boom-chick-a"** strum for each slash.

Here are a few songs written in tab. Sing along as you play them. Your voice provides the melody while the basic strum provides rhythmic backup.

Skip To My Lou

Lou,   Lou,   skip to my Lou,

Lou,   Lou,   skip to my Lou,

Lou,   Lou,   skip to my Lou,

Skip to my Lou, my   dar - ling.

Will the Circle be Unbroken

The basic strum sounds best when your index finger picks the keynote of each chord - the note that gives the chord its name. For example, the open third string is a G note, so pick the open third string when you strum a G chord. This series of grids tells you which are the keynotes of each chord.

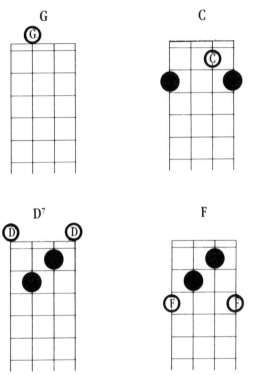

Strum each chord for a minute or two, always picking the keynote with your index finger. Then play the next two backup parts.

Buffalo Gals

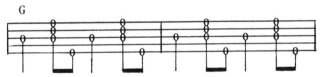

Buf-fa-lo gals, won't you come out to-night,

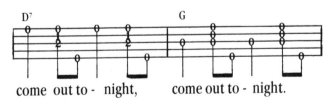

come out to-night,   come out to-night.

Buf-fa-lo gals, won't you come out to-night, we'll

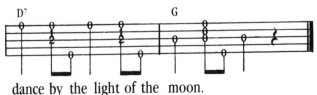

dance by the light of the moon.

20

Wabash Cannonball

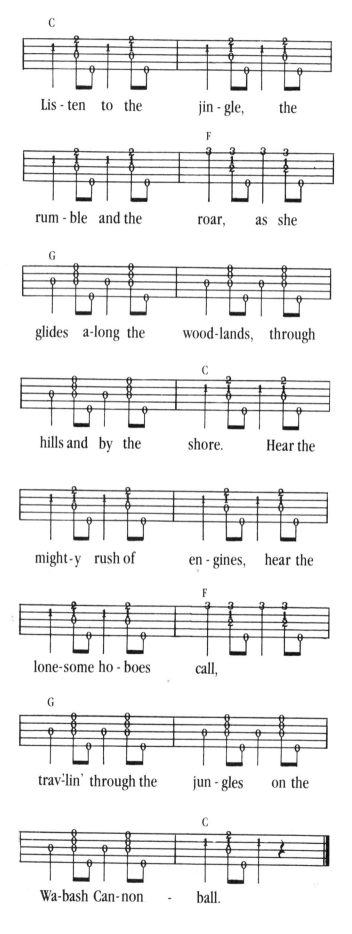

Alternating Notes with the Basic Strum

You can vary your basic strum backup by alternating between two notes with your index finger, like this:

Practice these measures over and over, as indicated by the **repeat signs:**

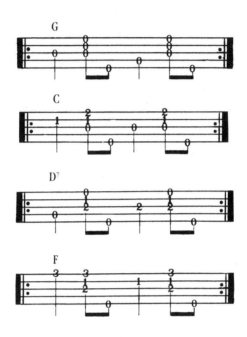

Buffalo Gals

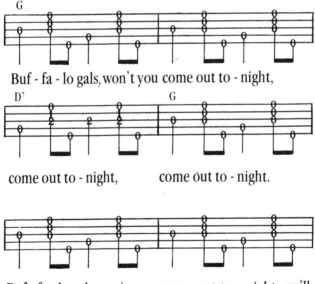

Buf - fa - lo gals, won't you come out to - night,

come out to - night,   come out to - night.

Buf - fa - lo gals, won't you come out to - night, we'll

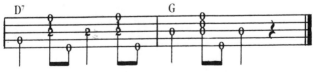

dance by the light of the moon.

Worried Man Blues

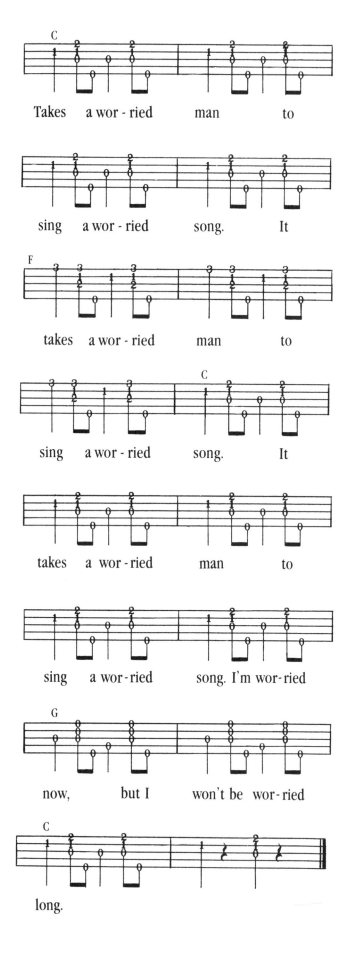

Hammering-on

Hammering-on means sounding a string by fretting it suddenly and forcibly with any finger of your left hand. Try it: pick the open third string, then quickly fret it at the 2nd fret with your middle finger/left hand. If you fret the string quickly and hard enough, a note will ring out almost as loud as if you had picked the string with your right hand.

Play these measures over and over. They show you how to use hammering-on to vary your basic strum backup. (Hammering-on is indicated in tab by the letter H.)

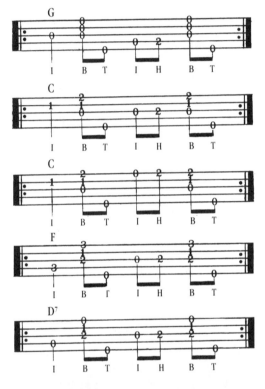

Now play this backup part. It's the basic strum with lots of hammering-on.

Red River Valley

Come and sit by my side if you love me. Do not has - ten to bid me a - dieu. Just re - mem - ber the Red Riv - er Val - ley, and the cow - boy who loves you so true.

Pulling-off

Pulling-off is plucking a string with any finger of your left hand. Try it: fret the first string, as shown in the picture, and pluck down. A note should sound, almost as loudly as if you had picked the string with your right hand.

Figure 12

Figure 13

Practice these basic strum measures. They include lots of pull-offs. (Pull-offs are indicated in tab by the letter P.)

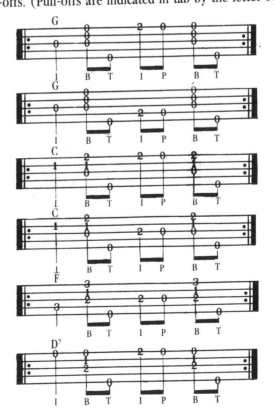

Now play this basic strum backup part. It includes pull-off and hammer-ons.

Worried Man Blues

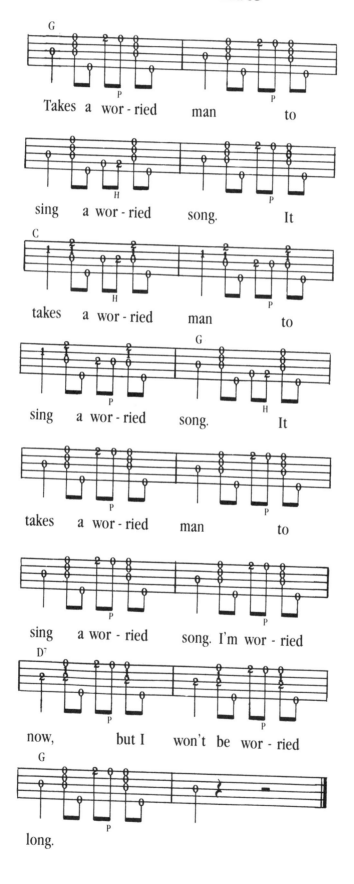

¾ Time

You can turn the basic strum into a ¾ (waltz time) strum by repeating the brush and thumb strokes. This gives you a **boom** - **chick-a** - **chick-a** rhythm.

boom - Index finger picks up on a single string.

Figure 14

chick -   Middle finger brushes down on first, second and third strings.

Figure 15

- **a** -   Thumb picks down on the fifth string. So far, you have done the basic strum.

Figure 16

chick -   Repeat step 2. (Brush down.)

Figure 17

- a-   Repeat step 3. (Thumb the fifth string.)

Figure 18

Play this ¾ strum over and over. The rhythm you want is:
boom - chick-a - chick-a, boom - chick-a - chick-a
1   2   3,   1   2   3

You can vary this ¾ time strum the same way you did the basic strum: add hammer-ons, pull-offs, and alternate index finger notes. Play these ¾ measures over and over:

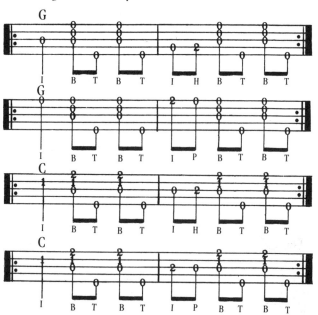

Play this waltz time backup part, and sing along as you play. It includes some basic strum embellishments hammer-ons and pull-offs.

Down in the Valley

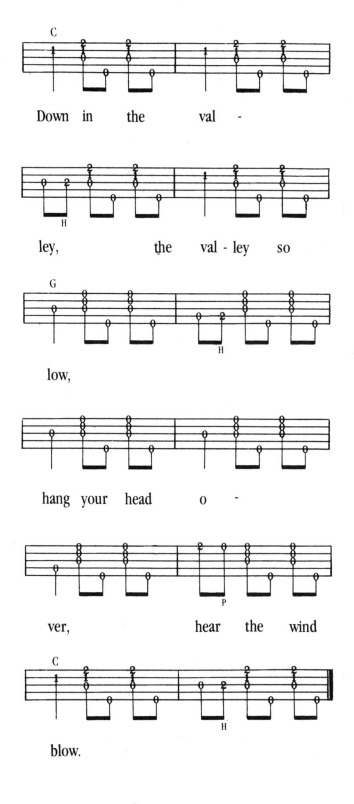

Clawhammer (Frailing) Style

Clawhammer style gets its name from the claw-like shape of the player's right hand. The technique, also called "old-time banjo," "frailing," "rapping" and "traditional banjo," probably came from Africa with the first banjos and was taught to white Southern mountain players by traveling black musicians. It precedes blue-grass banjo by at least one hundred and fifty years.

The technique is similar to the basic strum. It has the same **"boom-chick-a"** rhythm. Play these three strokes:

boom - Brush down with the nail of your index finger on the first string. Some players use their middle finger instead. (To distinguish it from the basic strum, this stroke will appear as M in the tab.)

Figure 19

chick - Brush down on all five strings (especially the first, second and third) with the nail of your index finger. If you used your middle finger for the first stroke, use it, for this stroke also.

Figure 20

- a - Pick down on the fifth string with your thumb.

Figure 21

Play these clawhammer style measures over and over, with a smooth "boom-chick-a" rhythm. As in the basic strum, there is a pause after the first stroke only. Another similarity: the first stroke isn't always on the first string; it can be on any string but the fifth; and it can be followed by a hammer-on or pull-off.

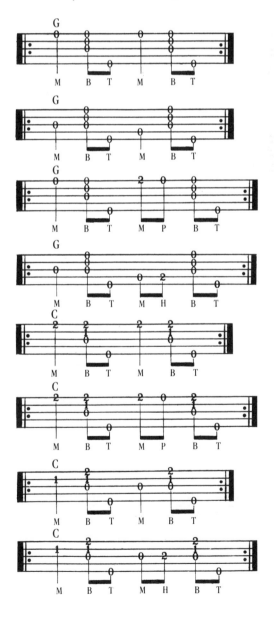

Go back to all the basic strum tunes and play them clawhammer style. Substitute M for I in the tab; otherwise, play them as written.

Picking Melodies

You can use the three-stroke clawhammer pattern to play melodies as well as backup. You play melody notes with the first stroke (index of middle finger, whichever is easier for you) and fill out the rhythm with the other two strokes. Here's an example:

Bile Them Cabbage Down

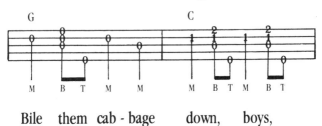

Bile them cab - bage down, boys,

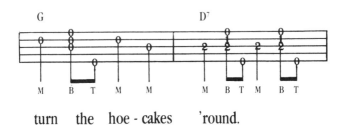

turn the hoe - cakes 'round.

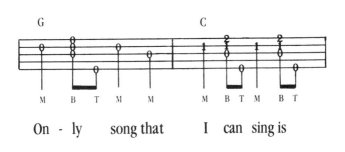

On - ly song that I can sing is

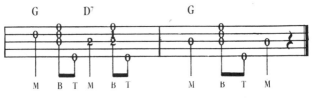

bile them cab - bage down.

The G and C Scales

A **scale** is a series of notes separated from each other by fixed intervals. A **major scale** is made up of eight notes: the eighth note has the same letter/name as the first note and is said to be an octave above it.

If a song is in the key of G, its melody is usually made up of notes from the G scale. Likewise, key of C tunes contain notes of the C scale. You will be able to pick melodies "off the top of your head" on the banjo if you're well aquainted with these two scales. Play a G chord, then play the G scale below, over and over, emphasizing the G notes. Then do the same with the C scale.

G Scale (fret a G chord)

C Scale (fret a C chord)

Once you can play the G and C scales forward and backward quickly and easily, try picking out some melodies on the banjo. Don't worry about strumming, chords or brush strokes, just try to play the bare melody. Strum a G chord and play the familiar nursery rhyme written below; then finish the melody yourself. Do the same in the key of C.

Mystery Nursery Rhyme

Key of G

Key of C

Use the same process with other familiar tunes. Play the starting chord (G or C), then hunt for the melody.

You've already played the backup part to this song; now you can play the melody, clawhammer style. Your index or middle finger plays the melody notes, and the "brush, thumb the fifth string" strokes fill out the rhythm.

Will the Circle be Unbroken

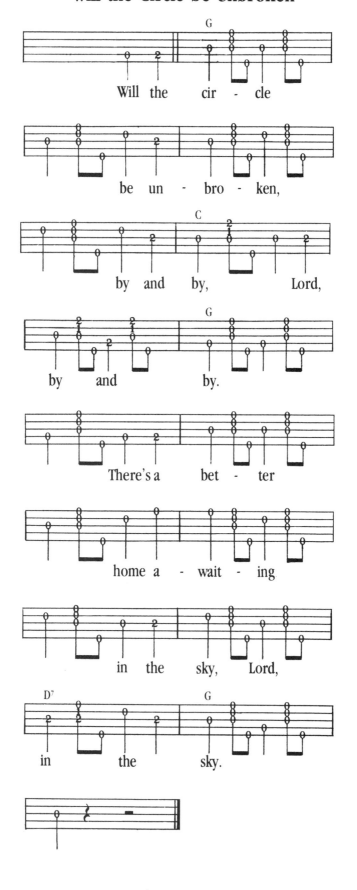

Banjo players have been frailing fiddle/banjo tunes like **"Old Joe Clark"** for many years. As in most of the old dance tunes, this arrangement has two parts; a verse and a chorus.

You'll be hammering-on and pulling-off in this tune, plus a new technique: **sliding.** Sliding is picking a fretted string and then moving your left hand up to a higher fret. Play the four slides written below. (A slide is indicated in tab by a line connecting two notes: .)

Figure 22

Old Joe Clark

Old Joe Clark, the preach-er's son,

preached all o - ver the plain. The

on - ly text he ev - er knew was

"high, low, Jack and the game."

'Round and 'round, Old Joe Clark,

'round and 'round I say. I'd

fol - low you ten thou - sand miles to

hear your ban - jo play.

Drop-thumb Frailing

A clawhammer banjo player is considered a virtuoso if he
or she can "keep up with" a fiddler and not leave out
any of the melody. The technique of drop-thumbing will
help you play all those grace notes and melodic
embellishments in a banjo/fiddle tune.

Play the two measures below, over and over, until you
can play them as smoothly and quickly as the three-
stroke clawhammer lick.

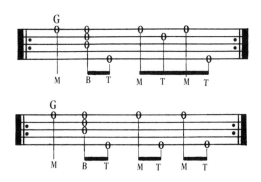

Bile Them Cabbage Down

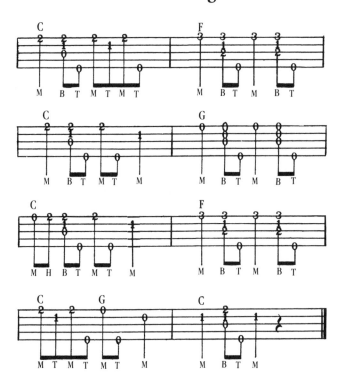

The clawhammer melodies you've played can also be
played with the basic strum. Go back and replay them,
putting in an I wherever there's an M in the tab. You'll
discover that sliding, hammering-on, pulling-off and
drop-thumbing can help you embellish the basic strum,
just as they did the clawhammer stroke.

Double-thumbing

Wearing Picks

Double-thumbing (sometimes called two-finger picking) is a fingerpicking technique that can be used for backup or melody playing. Most players who fingerpick wear a thumbpick and one or two fingerpicks. These picks make the banjo sound louder and clearer, and they save wear and tear on your fingers. You'll probably want to use them to play bluegrass banjo (three-finger picking), too.

Use a plastic thumbpick. They come in different sizes, so find one that fits your thumb snugly. However, use metal fingerpicks, which can be bent to fit your fingers.

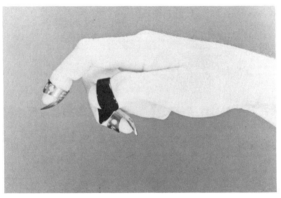

Figure 23

The fingerpicks help you pick **up** on the strings, so they are worn on the fleshy part of your finger. They are like backward fingernails!

Double-thumbing Licks

In double-thumbing, the thumb plays the main beats, instead of the index or middle fingers. The index finger "fills in" on higher strings. Here are some basic double-thumbing backup licks. Practice them over and over until you can play them quickly and smoothly.

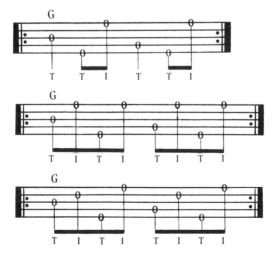

Little Birdie

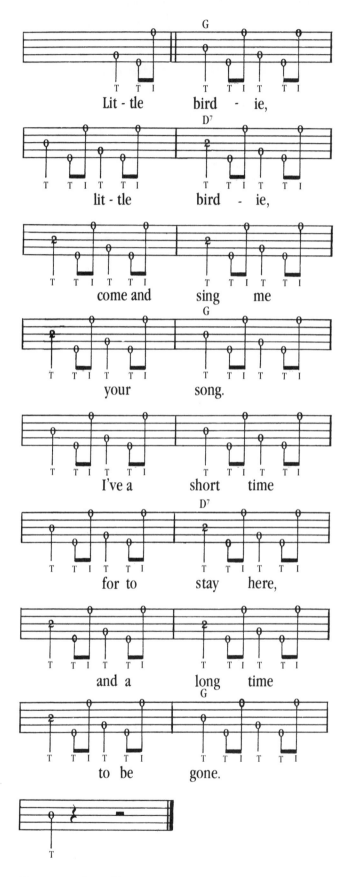

Connecting Runs

The next backup part uses **connecting runs.** A connecting run is a brief series of notes leading from one chord to another.

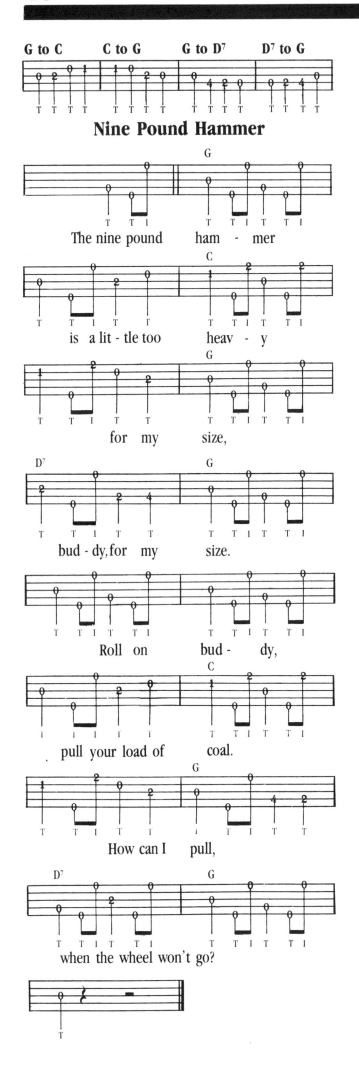

G to C   **C to G**   **G to D⁷**   **D⁷ to G**

Nine Pound Hammer

The nine pound ham - mer

is a lit - tle too heav - y

for my size,

bud - dy, for my size.

Roll on bud - dy,

pull your load of coal.

How can I pull,

when the wheel won't go?

Here is a double-thumbing arrangement in which the thumb plays melody. After learning it, try to make up similar parts for other tunes you've already strummed.

Nine Pound Hammer

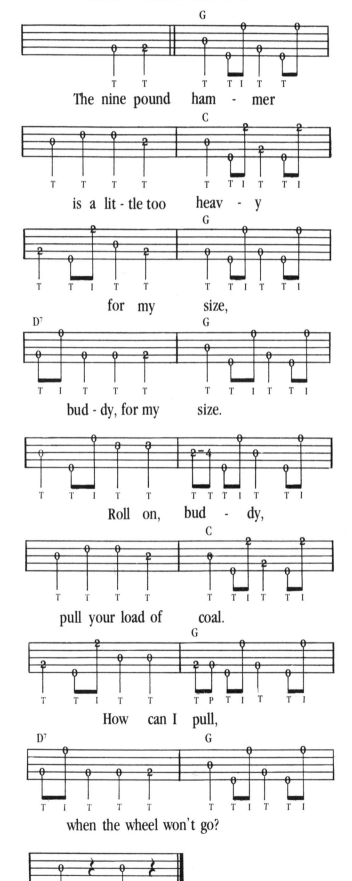

Bluegrass Banjo:
The "Scruggs Style"

In the early 1940's, Bill Monroe put together a string band that had a more streamlined sound than the mountain string bands, yet retained the flavor of mountain music more than the popular country ensembles of the time. Instrumentalists alternated taking "breaks" after every verse/chorus vocal, so there was plenty of room for the fiddler, banjoist and mandolinist to "show off." Because Monroe was from the bluegrass region of Kentucky, he called his group Bill Monroe and The Bluegrass Boys.

His sound jelled in the mid 1940's, with the addition of Earl Scruggs on the 5-string banjo. Scruggs had a speedy, syncopated, three-finger style of picking that had terrific drive and bounce. By the beginning of the 1950's bands that imitated Monroe's musical format proliferated in the South. Most included banjoists who played like Scruggs. The term Bluegrass Boys began to be applied to any group that had that sound.

The Right-hand Position

Bluegrass banjo players play melody and backup with rapid three-finger rolls. Learning to play these rolls quickly and smoothly is the key to bluegrass banjo.

In order to concentrate all your right-hand energy toward the thumb, index and middle fingers, stabilize your right hand on the banjo head as shown in this picture. Your pinkie and ring finger stay down on the banjo head all the time you're picking.

Figure 24

In bluegrass rolls, the middle finger usually plays the first string. The thumb plays five, four, three and sometimes two; the index finger plays four, three and two.

Position your right hand near the banjo bridge. The closer you are to the bridge, the more brittle and sharp you'll sound; as you pick farther from the brdge, your sound becomes more mellow and "plunky." Try picking a few notes at different distances from the bridge and see for yourself.

Three-finger Rolls

Practice the rolls below slowly, with an even rhythm. Speed them up gradually, but always keep the rhythm smooth. Every roll has eight beats; the emphasis should fall on the first and fifth beats (**one,** 2, 3, 4, **five,** 6, 7, 8.) Play each roll over and over, with no pause between repetitions.

Some of the rolls include hammer-ons, pull-offs or slides. Sometimes you'll be sounding two notes at once, by picking one string while hammering-on to another, or by sliding on one string while picking another.

Index Finger Lead Rolls (These are also called forward rolls.)

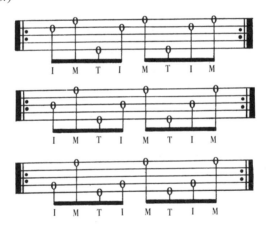

Thumb or Index Finger Lead Rolls

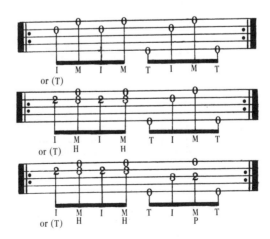

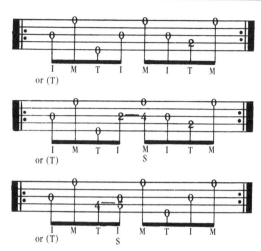

Thumb Lead Rolls (double-thumbing rolls)

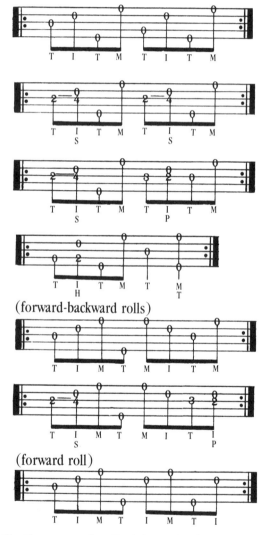

(forward-backward rolls)

(forward roll)

Middle Finger Lead Rolls (also called backwards rolls)

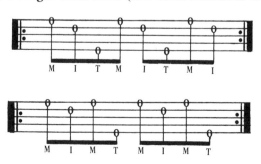

Some Bluegrass Arrangements

You double-thumbed **"Little Birdie"**; now play it "Scruggs style," using three-finger rolls. Notice how the first half is little more than melody with forward rolls for fill-in; the second half has thumb lead rolls playing melody.

Little Birdie

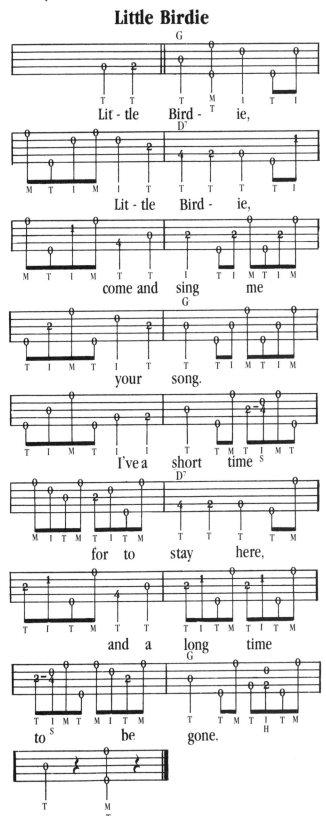

This version of **Bury Me Beneath the Willow** mixes
several types of rolls — index and thumb lead. It has
lots of bluegrass licks, including the opening "climb up
the second string," the second string hammer-on, and
the tag ending.

Bury Me Beneath the Willow

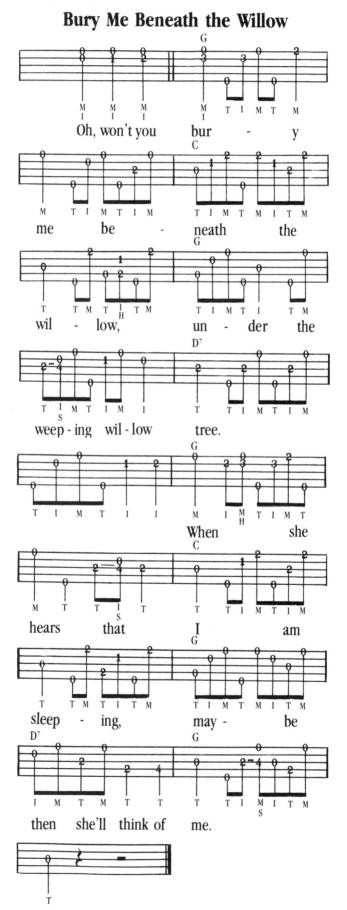

Bluegrass Backup

You can play a simple bluegrass backup by playing forward rolls and changing chords at the right time; add an occasional bass run, a tag ending, and your backup will sound professional!

Nine Pound Hammer

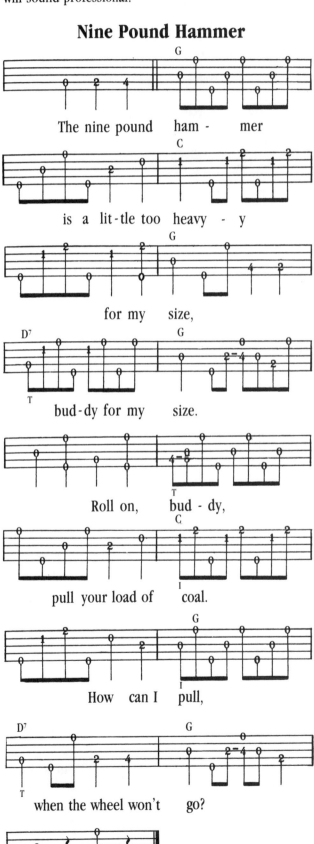

Here is another backup part. It contains slightly more varied rolls, and a hammer-on lick which makes good backup for a D or D⁷ chord:

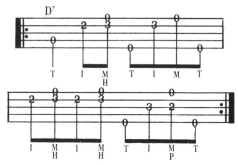

Bury Me Beneath the Willow

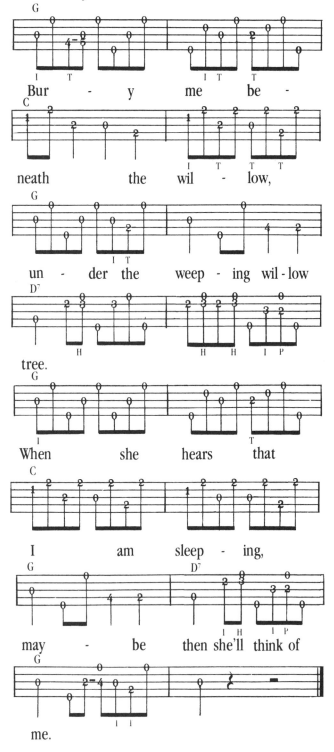

Playing Up the Neck

Movable Chords

The four movable chords pictured below are the key to playing "up the neck" of the banjo. They are called **"movable"** because you can move them up and down the fretboard. You already know the F formation; learn the others. Strum each one and move it to different places on the fretboard.

F formation

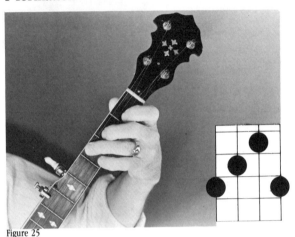

Figure 25

On the first fret (as pictured), this is an F chord. Move it up to the 3rd fret (index finger on the 3rd fret) and it becomes G. Learn these positions:
3rd fret: G   5th fret: A   8th fret: C   10th fret: D
15th fret: high G

Am formation

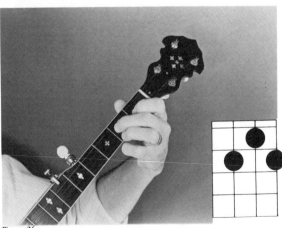

Figure 26

The A minor formation is like a C chord with the middle finger lowered to the third string. As you move the formation around the fretboard, do not pick the fourth string; since it's unfretted, it may clash with the other strings.
1st fret: Am   3rd fret: Bm   8th fret: Em

D formation

Figure 27

To switch from F formation to D formation, keep your ring finger and pinkie in place, and switch your index and middle fingers around; index on the third string, middle on the second string. Learn these positions:
2nd fret:D   5th fret: F   7th fret: G   9th fret: A
12th fret: C

Bar formation

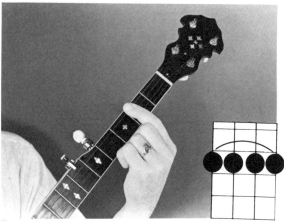

Figure 28

Fret all four strings with your index finger. Press hard so that all the strings ring out when you strum. Learn these positions:
2nd fret: A   4th fret: B   5th fret: C   7th fret: D
12th Fret: G

Chop Chords

You can deaden or mute a string by touching it, but not
fretting it, with your left hand. Try this: pick a fretted
string, then lift the fretting finger so that it just touches
the string. This stops the plucked string from ringing out.
If you pick a movable chord and quickly deaden it like
this, you have played a **chop chord**.

Chop chords are staccato (short sounding); you can use
them as a backup technique to accent the rhythm.
Bluegrass players play them on the upbeats (the third
and seventh beats of each measure) like this:

G (D formation)

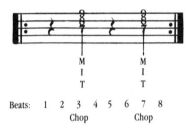

The thumb, index and middle fingers pick the chord;
sometimes the thumb picks the fourth string, instead of
the third.

Here's a chop chord backup to **"Wabash Cannonball!"** in the key of G. Sing along as you play it. Playing chop chords is a good way to practice the movable formations.

Wabash Cannonball

Playing in Different Keys

Using a Capo

A **capo** is a clamp made of rubber, metal and elastic, which clamps onto the fretboard and raises the pitch of all the strings. Many types of capos are available at music stores.

You can play a tune in the key of A by putting the capo on the 2nd fret, tuning the fifth string up to A (so that it matches the first string/7th fret, and playing the chords as if you were in G tuning.

To play in D: capo up two frets, tune the fifth string two frets higher than usual (to an A note) and play as if you were playing a key of C tune in G tuning.

To play in E: capo up four frets, retune the fifth string to G# (one fret higher than usual) and play as if you were playing a key of C tune in G tuning.

To play in F: the same as E, but one fret higher (both the capo and the fifth string).

To play in B^b: the same as A, only one fret higher.

To play in B: the same as A, only two frets higher.

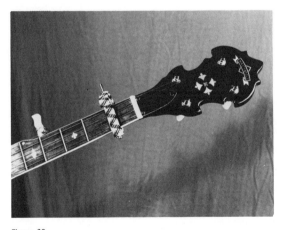

Figure 29

C Tuning: G C G B D

"Old-time" or **"traditional"** banjo players who play the older mountain styles of music use several different tunings. Each tuning has a musical flavor all its own, and a set of chords and licks; and some tunes are traditionally played in certain tunings.

C tuning is probably the most widespread, popular tuning . . . second only to the G tuning. It's the same as G tuning except for the fourth string, which is tuned down to a low C. This low C comes in handy when you play in the key of C!

To get into C tuning, fret the second string/1st fret, and tune the fourth string down to match it; it will become a C note an octave lower.

C tuning chords are just like G tuning chords, except for the fourth string:

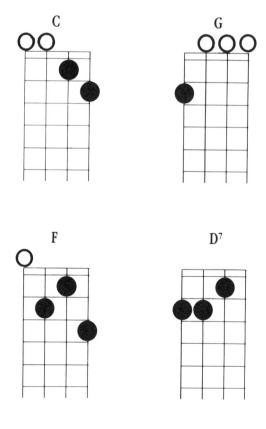

C   G

F   D⁷

Soldier's Joy is a very old and popular fiddle/banjo tune. This clawhammer arrangement includes some drop-thumbing. This C chord is used in this song:

Soldier's Joy

"C Tuning"

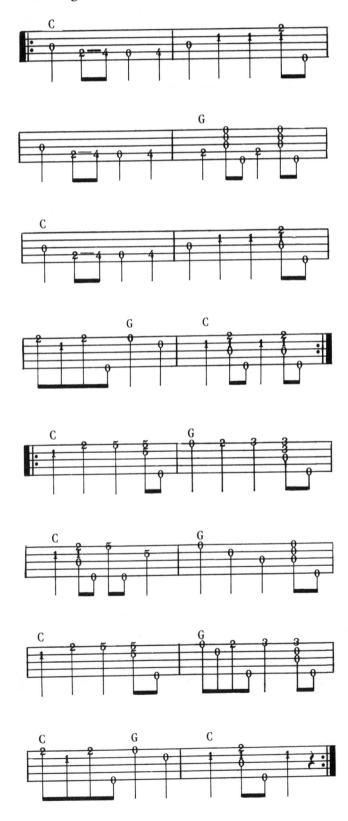

More Chords

A lot of songs contain more than three or four chords. Here are some useful additions to your G tuning chord vocabulary:

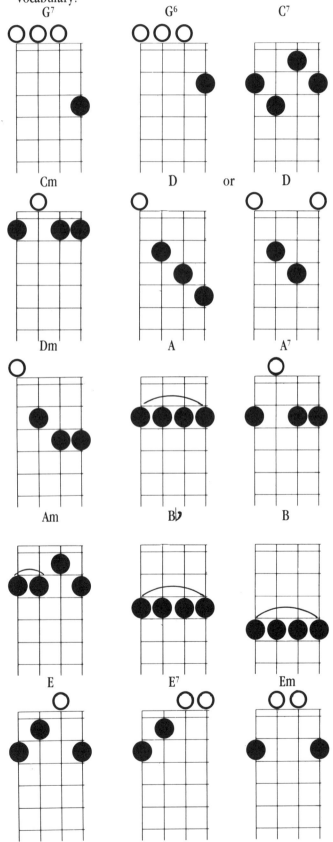

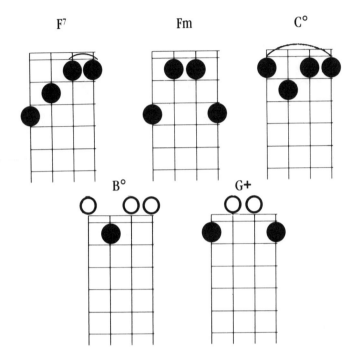

Discography

Listen to the banjo masters. Go see them perform whenever possible; besides being a lot of fun, this is one of the best ways to learn. The next best thing is listening to their records. Here are some names to look for:

Clawhammer Style:

Wade Ward
Kyle Creed
Fred Cockerham (on fiddler Tommy Jarrell lps)
Clarence Ashley (on early Doc Watson lps)
Grandpa Jones (seen on Hee-Haw TV show sometimes)

Double-Thumbing and Two Finger Picking Style:

Roscoe Holcomb
Bascom Lamar Lunsford
Uncle Dave Macon
Pete Steele
Stringbean (Dave Akeman)

Basic Strum:

Pete Seeger (his own and The Weavers lps)
The Kingston Trio
The Limeliters

Bluegrass:

Earl Scruggs (especially early Flatt and Scruggs lps)
Ralph Stanley (his own and Stanley Brothers lps)
Don Reno (his own and Reno and Smiley lps)

Melodic and Newgrass Style:

Bill Keith (fiddle tunes, swing)
Alan Munde (fiddle tunes, swing)
Tony Trischka (sometimes plays with drums, horns, etc.)
Bela Fleck (very experimental newgrass picking)
Pat Cloud (a jazz banjo player)
Fred Sokolow (melodic arrangements of ragtime music)
Pete Wernick (banjo with phase shifter!)
Fred Geiger (melodic versions of early swing music)

Other Banjo Books From Music Sales

How To Play Banjo	Jim Jumper	AM35155
Bluegrass Banjo	Peter Wernick	OK62778
How To Play The 5-String Banjo	Pete Seeger	OK61291
Hot Licks For Bluegrass Banjo	Tony Trischka	OK63909
Teach Yourself Bluegrass Banjo	Tony Trischka	AM21593
Original Banjo Case Chord Book	Tony Trischka	AM34885
Melodic Clawhammer Banjo	Ken Pearlman	OK63644
Clawhammer Banjo	Miles Krassen	OK63016
Melodic Banjo	Tony Trischka	OK63149
Banjo Songbook	Tony Trischka	OK63438

About The Author

Fred Sokolow plays everything from bluegrass to Bo Diddley and can be seen often playing jazz guitar in L.A. night spots, 5-string banjo at bluegrass festivals, and he's just as likely to turn up at studio sessions playing rock guitar. You may even spot him playing dobro or mandolin on those wonderful folk revivals seen on cable and public television.

Fred has played in such diverse clubs and concert halls as the Electric Circus in New York, the Fillmore Auditorium in San Francisco, the Aladdin Hotel in Las Vegas, the Denver Folklore Center and Donte's Jazz Club in Los Angeles. He has toured worldwide with artists such as Bobbie Gentry, Jim Stafford, and The Limeliters, always armed with an arsenal of varied instruments.

There are two bluegrass banjo and two rock guitar LPs available showcasing Fred's incredible technique, both of which received excellent reviews in the U.S. and Europe. In addition, he has written dozens of instructional guitar and banjo books for seven major publishers. His books, which teach jazz, rock, country, and bluegrass technique, are sold on six continents!

As articulate in person as he is in print, Fred presents guitar and banjo seminars across the U.S. You can read reviews of these seminars, as well as on his instructional books and tapes (including video), in *Guitar Player, Frets,* and other music magazines. He is a frequent contributor to *Banjo Newsletter,* and can be heard on television and radio talk shows promoting his seminars and books.

If you still think that Fred isn't versatile enough, know that in his early days he M.C.'d for Carol Doda at San Francisco's legendary Condor Club, accompanied a Russian balalaika virtuoso for a month at L.A.'s swank Bonaventure hotel, won *The Gong Show,* and wrote and performed the score for the movie "Rampaging Nurses"!

—Ronnie Schiff